Note to parents, carers and teachers

Read it yourself is a series of modern stories, favourite characters, traditional tales and first reference books written in a simple way for children who are learning to read. The books can be read independently or as part of a guided reading session.

Each book is carefully structured to include many high-frequency words vital for first reading. The sentences on each page are supported closely by pictures to help with understanding, and to offer lively details to talk about.

The books are graded into four levels that progressively introduce wider vocabulary and longer text as a reader's ability and confidence grows.

Ideas for use

- Begin by looking through the book and talking about the pictures. Has your child heard this story or looked at this subject before?

- Help your child with any words he does not know, either by helping him to sound them out or supplying them yourself.

- Developing readers can be concentrating so hard on the words that they sometimes don't fully grasp the meaning of what they're reading. Answering the quiz questions at the end of the book will help with understanding.

For more information and advice on Read it yourself and book banding, visit **www.ladybird.com/readityourself**

Book Band 5

Level 1 is ideal for children who have received some initial reading instruction. Stories are told, or subjects are presented very simply, using a small number of frequently repeated words.

Special features:

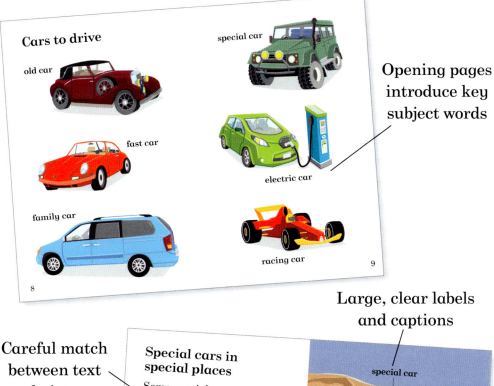

Cars to drive

old car

special car

fast car

electric car

family car

racing car

Opening pages introduce key subject words

8

9

Large, clear labels and captions

Careful match between text and pictures

Special cars in special places

Some special cars can drive in many different places.

special car

Would you like to drive here?

20

21

Educational Consultant: Geraldine Taylor
Book Banding Consultant: Kate Ruttle
Subject Consultant: Chris Woodford

LADYBIRD BOOKS

UK | USA | Canada | Ireland | Australia
India | New Zealand | South Africa

Ladybird Books is part of the Penguin Random House group of companies
whose addresses can be found at global.penguinrandomhouse.com.

www.penguin.co.uk   www.puffin.co.uk   www.ladybird.co.uk

First published 2016
This edition 2019
002

Copyright © Ladybird Books Ltd, 2016

Printed in China

A CIP catalogue record for this book is available from the British Library

ISBN: 978-0-241-40540-6

All correspondence to:
Ladybird Books
Penguin Random House Children's
One Embassy Gardens, 8 Viaduct Gardens, London SW11 7BW

Cars

Written by Catherine Baker
Illustrated by Jenna Riggs

Contents

Cars to drive

old car

fast car

family car

special car

electric car

racing car

I love cars!

There are so many different cars to drive.

I am a racing driver. I love to drive cars!

Old cars

These cars are very old.

They do not go very fast.

old car

Big cars

Some cars are very big.

Would you like to go in this car?

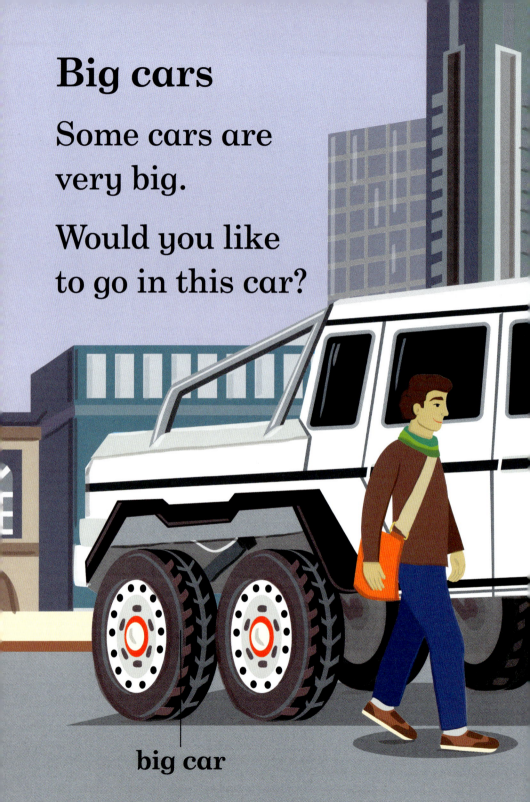

big car

15

Little cars

Have you seen little cars like these?

little car

17

Family cars

Do you have a car in your family?

Is your car like this one?

Special cars in special places

Some special cars can drive in many different places.

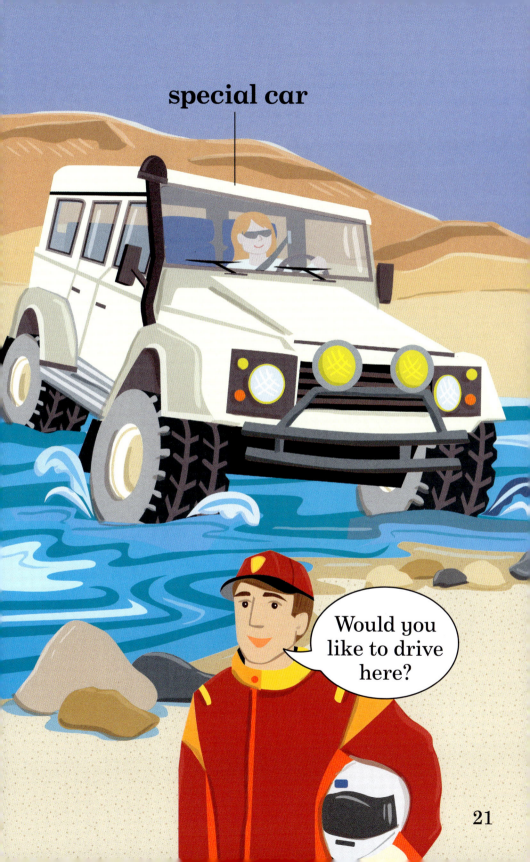

21

Petrol cars, electric cars

Many cars need petrol
so they can go.

petrol car

These cars are different.
They do not need petrol.
They are electric.

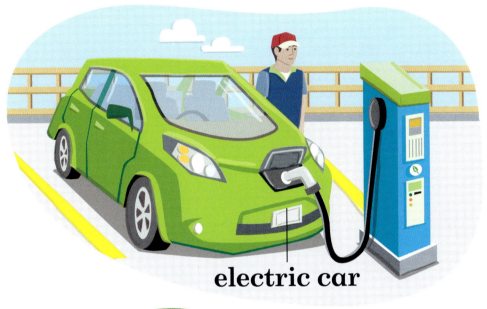

electric car

This electric car is going fast!

Fast cars

There are some very fast cars here!

—— **fast car**

Racing cars

Only racing drivers can drive these very fast cars.

racing car

I am going to drive one of these fast racing cars!

Picture glossary

 big car

 electric car

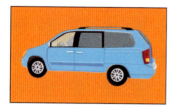 family car

 fast car

 little car

 old car

 petrol car

 racing car

 racing driver

 special car

Index

Cars quiz

What have you learnt about cars?
Answer these questions and find out!

- ## Which cars do not go very fast?

- ## What do cars need to make them go?

- ## Who can drive a racing car?

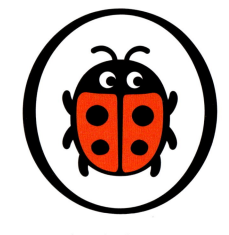

www.ladybird.com